GLADIATOR

ᴀɴ GIBBONS & ROBBIE GIBBONS

Illustrated by

CHAPTER 1

I found the helmet on a beach in Italy. We were on holiday. I'd gone for a walk with Dad and I had run ahead. The old man never could keep up with me. I tripped over something and fell. When I looked back, there it was, sticking out of the sand.

I dusted it off. It was badly rusted. Anyone else might have thought it was an old piece of junk, but not me. My skin was prickling. I had found something important.

I imagined a soldier wearing it to battle thousands of years ago. I could hear Dad calling me, but I didn't answer. All I could focus on was the helmet.

I put it on, just to see how it felt, but it was too big for me. It slipped down over my face so I couldn't see through the eyeholes. Inside, the helmet was dark and stuffy. I couldn't see a thing. The sounds of the waves and the sea breeze had suddenly stopped. I got this weird feeling, like the air was bending around me. Like the ground was shifting under my feet.

When I took the helmet off, everything had changed. I wasn't on a white, sunny beach any more. I was in a narrow tunnel. It was gloomy and full of shadows. The air reeked of stale sweat and body odour. There was a steel gate ahead of me. Light drifted in through the gaps in it. I was alone, but I could hear the rumble of distant voices. Where was I?

Then I noticed something.

The helmet in my hands was no longer rusty. It was brand new, as shiny as silver.

I heard a cough. I wasn't alone. I looked up to see a man watching me. His eyes gleamed in the shadows.

"You're next, gladiator," he said. He tossed me a shield. "You'll need this."

Gladiator?

I looked at the shield and caught my reflection in its surface. I was a fully grown adult, with dark, straggly hair and olive-green eyes. My body was covered by a shining breastplate, marked by the dents and scratches of past battles.

While I studied the new me, the man disappeared through a doorway and a lock clicked into place behind him.

"Good luck," I heard him mutter. I had a feeling I was going to need it.

CHAPTER 2

Chains rattled. The gate lurched upwards and light poured in from above. There was nowhere else to go.

I made my way to the end of the tunnel, slitting my eyes against the brightness of the sun. I could hear excited whispers. The whispers rose to cheers as I stepped out into the light.

The arena was round and covered in gritty sand that crunched beneath my feet. Above the arena walls there was a cursing, yelling, clapping, screaming crowd of people. It reminded me of the time my dad had taken me to watch a football match in the Nou Camp.

I raised my arms and a cheer rose with them, as loud as thunder. I smiled. They loved me. I was a celebrity.

I was a gladiator.

When the gate on the other side of the arena screeched open, my smile vanished. Out of the shadows stepped the biggest man I'd ever seen. His arms were huge and criss-crossed with scars. His chest was bare, as if his skin was so thick he had no need for armour. His face was cut in half by another ragged scar. It twisted his mouth into a cruel smile.

Who was I kidding? I wasn't a gladiator. *That* was a gladiator.

He unsheathed his sword. The sound was like paper tearing. I imagined that sword tearing through my flesh. A shudder ran through my body. I had to get out of there.

I looked back at the gate. It was closed. I was so distracted by the cheers that I hadn't heard it slam shut behind me. The arena wall was about five metres high, too high for even my new self to reach. There was no escape.

Then it hit me – the helmet. I still held it in the crook of my elbow. That's how I got here, so maybe I could go back the same way? I tried to put it on, but in my panic it slipped through my shaking fingers. Before I could pick it up, the gladiator swiped it away with his sword, sending it clattering across the arena floor.

"Draw your weapon, coward."

I needed the helmet. It had landed somewhere behind me. I wanted to make a run for it, but I didn't dare turn my back on this man, not even for a second. I had no choice.

CHAPTER 3

I pulled my sword from its sheath and tested its weight. It felt familiar, as if I had used it before. The giant gladiator swung his sword at me and before I knew what I was doing, I had raised my own to meet it. The blades clashed, sending shockwaves down my arm.

The crowd cheered. I realised that I didn't just look like a gladiator. I had a gladiator's skills. Confidence pumped through me, steadying my shaking hands.

Our eyes locked as we circled each other slowly. My enemy's sword was twice the size of my short stabbing sword. It looked twice as deadly, but it was heavy, too, and he had to hold it with both hands. At least my smaller weapon gave me the advantage of quick movement. I could do this. All I had to do was hold him off long enough to get the helmet.

He came at me again. His sword sliced the air. I ducked and weaved beneath his blows. One of them nearly got me. It hissed so close to my face that I felt the cold rush of air. This wasn't going to be easy.

I kept my guard up and let the rhythm of the
fight drive me forward. It was a close match.
The crowd fell quiet and edged forward to get a
better view.

We traded strike after strike. The clang of our blades echoed around the hushed arena. I was starting to get out of breath. Sweat poured down my face. It stung my eyes and left a salty taste on my lips. Every few seconds I risked a sideways glance towards the helmet, but I couldn't see it.

The gladiator knew I was distracted. He lunged at me and caught me by surprise. I tried to block, but it was no use. As he raised his sword, the blade caught the sun and blinded me for a split second. It was a split second I couldn't afford to lose.

He aimed for my weak point, the bare flesh under my arm-guard. The blade connected. It cut deep, tearing through skin and muscle. I screamed so hard that my neck tightened and my voice broke. My blood dripped freely and stained the sand with pearls of crimson.

My strength was seeping out of me. My courage went with it. I tried to lift my sword arm, but it was no use. My weapon dropped uselessly to the ground. The gladiator grinned. He knew he'd cornered his prey.

He kicked my sword out of reach and punched me to the ground. I choked on sand. I tasted blood on my swollen lips.

That's when I saw it, glinting in the corner of my eye – the helmet! It was only a few inches away from my good hand but I couldn't quite reach it.

The gladiator stood over me. He raised his sword over my neck like an executioner. I squeezed my eyes shut, waiting for a blow that never came. What was he waiting for?

I followed his gaze. He was looking at a man sitting in a special box in the crowd – the Emperor. The gladiator was waiting for the Emperor to give his decision. Thumbs up, I lived. Thumbs down, I died. My fate was about to be decided by a twitch of his hand. Would it be life or death?

I wasn't planning on sticking around long enough to find out. I reached for the helmet, stretching so hard that I thought my arms might pop out of their sockets. I felt the cold metal on my fingertips. Just a little further …

All eyes were on the Emperor.

"Kill, kill, kill," the crowd cried. The same mob who had cheered me was now roaring for my blood. I managed to curl a fingertip inside of the helmet. I was so close, but my time was up. The Emperor twisted his wrist.

Thumbs down.

Game over.

With my last ounce of strength, I hooked my whole finger inside the helmet and dragged it towards me. It rattled over the sandy arena floor.

The gladiator bent his knees and lifted his sword high …

I gripped the helmet with both hands, lifted it up and pulled it down over my head.

At the same time, the gladiator dropped his sword. I heard it rasp towards me. My scream echoed inside the helmet.

Nothing happened. The crowd fell suddenly silent. The shouting stopped. Was I dead? I felt my neck. It was still in one piece – a good start. My hands moved upwards and I pulled the helmet off.

The sunlight was bright in my eyes. I could hear waves lapping the shore. I was back on the beach, with nothing but the white sand stretching out in every direction.

CHAPTER 4

Dad was still calling my name, just as he had been when I first put the helmet on. It was as if I had only been gone for a moment.

What should I do? Should I tell Dad what had happened? No, he was never going to believe me, and I certainly wasn't willing to put the helmet back on to prove it.

I quickly buried the helmet where I had found it. Dad caught up. He was out of breath.

"Legs aren't what they used to be," he panted. His forehead creased into a frown. "What on earth happened to your arm?"

I looked down. The sleeve of my T-shirt was soaked with dark blood where the gladiator had cut me.

Dad peeled the sleeve up and winced. "That looks nasty. We might have to take you to hospital. What happened?"

The helmet was what happened. The pain had been real. The damage was permanent.

Part of the helmet was still sticking out of the sand. That thing was dangerous. Anyone could trip and find it, just like I did, and end up in a fight to the death.

I had managed to get the helmet back on just in time to save my neck. The next guy might not be so lucky.

"I fell and cut myself on that old piece of junk," I said, pointing at the helmet. "We'd better bury it first, somewhere deep." My voice was serious. "So no one else gets hurt."

THE END

Tough fighting men

The ancient Roman world was a brutal one – and not just for gladiators. Read on to find out more about the real gladiators and other fighting men in Roman times.

Most gladiators were slaves or enemy soldiers that the Roman army had taken prisoner.

Gladiators fought in an **amphitheatre**. This was a huge, oval space with a sandy floor. The sand helped the gladiators grip with their bare feet. It also soaked up the blood.

The Emperor sat in a box at the North end.

The seats nearest the front were reserved for the wealthy.

Hidden lifts and trapdoors let gladiators and animals in from underground.

A single fight usually lasted for ten to fifteen minutes, and gladiators only fought a few times a year. Huge crowds went to watch the fights.

A gladiator was expected to die well. He must not beg for his life or cry out. If he lost and the crowd wanted him to die, he had to kneel and look up at the winner.

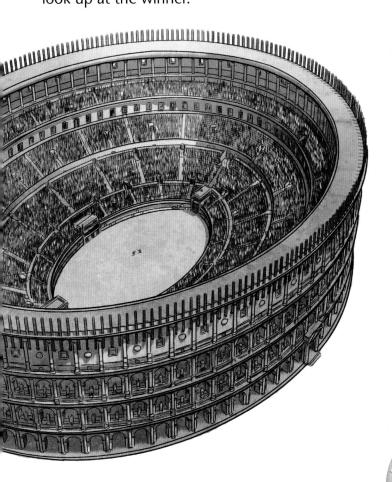

The gladiator showed his throat so the other man could drive his sword through the soft part and into his heart. That way he died quickly.

Few gladiators lasted more than ten bouts. Most died before they were thirty.

A popular gladiator with many fights behind him could win his freedom. He was then given a wooden sword to show he was a free man. Some gladiators earned their freedom, but still returned to fight.

Sometimes the slaves and gladiators rebelled. Spartacus led the best-known rebellion. His rebel army fought Roman soldiers for two years.

Marcus the Roman soldier

Roman soldiers were very tough fighters.

Take a look at Marcus. He is a Roman soldier, the kind that fought Spartacus. See his shoes? Do you think wearing sandals makes him a wimp? Think again. This is one of the bravest fighting men in history.

Let's start with those sandals. They're not the kind of shoes you wear on the beach. They're marching boots. There are **hobnails** in the soles. Nails are hammered through the soles to stop the leather wearing out. Soldiers might march twenty miles in a day.

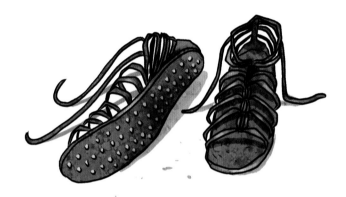

The hobnails have another purpose, too. They can come in useful in a fight. If one of Marcus's enemies slips or falls to the ground, he can stamp on his head and crack his skull.

Ouch!

Marcus wears a perfect piece of fighting kit.

He has a linen undershirt and a tunic made of wool.

Over the undershirt and tunic, he has body armour made of metal strips. This covers his chest, back and shoulders.

His helmet protects his forehead, neck and cheeks.

Some of Marcus's enemies have to fight without armour. He has a big advantage over them.

Marcus has to be strong. He carries a lot of gear. He has enough food for three days, a water bottle, cooking and digging tools, a cloak for bad weather and some spare clothes. This pack weighs around thirty kilos, about the same as the pack today's soldiers have to carry.

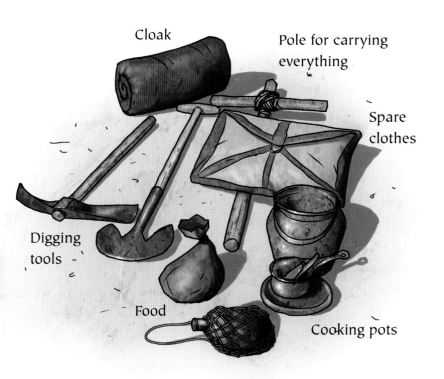

Cloak

Pole for carrying everything

Spare clothes

Digging tools

Food

Cooking pots

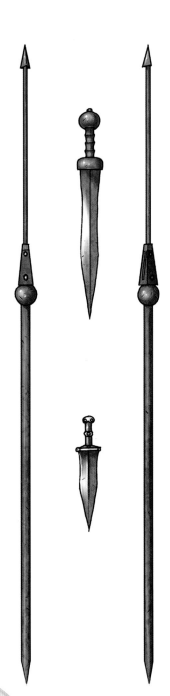

Then there are his
weapons. Marcus has
a light, short sword.
He doesn't wave it
around. He uses it to
stab his enemies. It's fast.
It's deadly.

The next weapon is the
javelin. Marcus has two
of them. When his javelin
sticks in an enemy shield,
it bends, so the enemy
can't throw it back.
He has a small dagger,
too. You don't mess
with Marcus.

Marcus is fit. As well as all the marching, he has to do weapons training every morning with dummy, wooden weapons. Many of the training swords are heavier than the ones used in battle. If a soldier can use the dummy weapon, he'll find the real thing easy. Then there's running, jumping and swimming, too. With all that marching and training, a Roman soldier is ready for anything.

In battle Marcus works with the man next to him. They lock shields to make a defensive wall. He braces himself against his shield so he can take the shock of an enemy attack. The soldiers can form a tortoise with a "shell" of shields all around them and on top. This totally protects them from the enemy.

Marcus always obeys orders. If he doesn't, his commander can give out terrible punishments.

The worst is called **decimation**. If any soldier runs away or doesn't fight hard enough, his unit is divided into groups of ten. The men draw lots. Nine of the men have to club the tenth man to death, even if he is one of their mates.

Another terrible Roman punishment is **crucifixion**. They save this one for slaves, pirates and the army's worst enemies. It means whipping somebody until their blood runs, making them weak. They then nail the victim to a wooden cross.

The Roman army once crucified six thousand slaves on the long road from Capua to Rome.

The Roman Empire became enormous, thanks to soldiers like Marcus. It once reached from Britain to the Middle East, and from Germany to Africa.

Men like Marcus were not afraid to kill without mercy if they had to. And they enjoyed watching the gladiators die.

It was a tough world – tough for the Roman soldiers and tough for the gladiators.

Trier ·

Lyons
·

Nimes ·

Rome · Split
·
· Capua

Antioch
·

Jerusalem
·

Alexandria
·

Memphis ·

THE ROMAN EMPIRE

Reader challenge

Word hunt

1 On page 5, find an adjective that means "dark".

2 On page 19, find a verb that means "pounced".

3 On page 45, find an adjective that means "huge".

Text sense

4 How do the author describe the amphitheatre? (page 32)

5 How did Marcus's clothes help him when he is fighting? (pages 37–38)

6 What does Marcus do to keep fit? (page 41)

7 How do you think a gladiator felt when he had to club one of his own men to death? (page 43)

8 Why did men like Marcus enjoy watching the gladiators die? (page 45)

Your views

9 What did you find more interesting, the information about the soldier or the information about the gladiator? Give reasons.

10 Would you like to have been a gladiator? Give reasons.

Spell it

With a partner, look at these words and then cover them up.

- beach
- shield
- blood

Take it in turns for one of you to read the words aloud. The other person has to try and spell each word. Check your answers, then swap over.

Try it

With a partner, imagine you are acting out part of the *Gladiator* story. Make a freeze-frame of the fight.

William Collins's dream of knowledge for all began with the publication of his first book in 1819. A self-educated mill worker, he not only enriched millions of lives, but also founded a flourishing publishing house. Today, staying true to this spirit, Collins books are packed with inspiration, innovation and practical expertise. They place you at the centre of a world of possibility and give you exactly what you need to explore it.

Collins. Freedom to teach.

Published by Collins Education
An imprint of HarperCollins*Publishers*
77–85 Fulham Palace Road
Hammersmith
London
W6 8JB

Browse the complete Collins Education catalogue at **www.collinseducation.com**

Text by Alan Gibbons and Robbie Gibbons © HarperCollins*Publishers* Limited 2012
Illustrations by Matt Timson © HarperCollins Publishers Limited 2012

Series consultants: Alan Gibbons and Natalie Packer

10 9 8 7 6 5 4 3 2 1
ISBN 978-0-00-746483-8

British Library Cataloguing in Publication Data.
A catalogue record for this publication is available from the British Library.

Commissioned by Catherine Martin
Edited and project-managed by Sue Chapple
Illustration management by Tim Satterthwaite
Proofreading by Grace Glendinning
Design and typesetting by Jordan Publishing Design Limited
Cover design by Paul Manning

Acknowledgements

The publishers would like to thank the students and teachers of the following schools for their help in trialling the Read On series:

Southfields Academy, London
Queensbury School, Queensbury, Bradford
Langham C of E Primary School, Langham, Rutland
Ratton School, Eastbourne, East Sussex
Northfleet School for Girls, North Fleet, Kent
Westergate Community School, Chichester, West Sussex
Bottesford C of E Primary School, Bottesford, Nottinghamshire
Woodfield Academy, Redditch, Worcestershire
St Richard's Catholic College, Bexhill, East Sussex